The Trump Resolution

*Spiritual Interview with
the Guardian Spirit of
Donald Trump*

RYUHO OKAWA

HS PRESS

Contents

Preface

In the end of this April, suddenly, a conference between the top leaders of North and South Koreas was held, and they talked about denuclearization and unification of the Korean Peninsula.

Many statesmen and people of mass media are welcoming this peace-making policy through the conversation. But we must know the fact that the maps used in North Korea do not have South Korea in the first place and they only have "Democratic People's Republic of Korea" in the Korean Peninsula. So, this North-South conference means that they officially admitted that there are two countries in the Korean Peninsula.

President Trump of America is, to some extent, evaluating the movement toward peace, but he must be preparing some strategies for the coming U.S.-North Korea conference. This book shows his strong resolution that if North Korea do not approve they are losers, "There will be no peace, prosperity, or unification between the North and the

South." At the same time, to Japan, his message is, "Be a sovereign country with strong leadership." To the idle diet and some of the mass media that's just saying what sounds good to the ears to escape responsibility, this book will give a good scolding.

Ryuho Okawa
Master & CEO of Happy Science Group
May 8, 2018

The Trump Resolution

Spiritual Interview with
the Guardian Spirit of Donald Trump

Recorded April 28, 2018
Happy Science General Headquarters,
Japan

Donald Trump (1946-Present)

The 45th president of the United States. Republican. Born in New York City. After graduating from the University of Pennsylvania in 1968, he began to work at his father's real estate company and was given control of the company in 1971. Caught the media's attention upon completing the Trump Tower on Fifth Avenue in New York in 1983, a building some people call to be the most expensive in the world. Trump is known as a real estate magnate, making millions and billions due to his great success in real estate development, and hotel and casino management. His autobiography published when he was 41 years old became a bestseller. He has also published many works on success theory. Trump had appeared many times in the media as a TV personality. Made his presidential announcement in June 2015. With "Make America Great Again" as his slogan, Trump attracted large numbers of supporters and won the hard-fought presidential election in 2016.

Interviewers from Happy Science*:

Kazuhiro Ichikawa
Senior Managing Director
Chief Director of International Headquarters

Kiyoshi Shimada
Director General in Training of International El Cantare-belief
Promotion Division

Jiro Ayaori
Managing Director
Director General of Magazine Editing Division
Chief Editor of *The Liberty*
Lecturer, Happy Science University

*No statements made by the guardian spirit of Donald Trump in this book
reflect statements actually made by Donald Trump himself.*

*The opinions of the spirit do not necessarily reflect those of Happy Science Group. For
the mechanism behind spiritual messages, see end section.*

* Interviewers are listed in the order that they appear in the transcript. Their
professional titles represent their positions at the time of the interview.

1

Attempting to Uncover President Trump's True Thoughts Before the U.S.-North Korea Conference

RYUHO OKAWA

As you know, yesterday, we saw a historical event; the North and South Korea conference. It was a sudden event and no one could expect that event, so we just want to know what the real thinking of Mr. Donald Trump is.

This morning, I talked with his guardian spirit and he said, "It's top-secret. Top-secret is top-secret, but if you, Happy Science, want to know something, there is some way to show what he is really thinking about; it's how you approach me." He said so.

So, to tell the truth, it will be a very difficult matter. He cannot show every card he has now before the next conference between Kim Jong-un and Donald Trump. It's diplomacy. So, he can't reveal everything. He must hide something, especially, what he really thinks about the conclusion of the meeting.

But today, we have this opportunity to hear from him. Even the American journalists or TV casters, including CNN, cannot interview him, especially his real thinking. Adding to that, I must say today's session is not the real Donald Trump, but his guardian spirit's opinion.

His guardian spirit wants to speak in English, so from our reading, it may be the first American president, George Washington. [See Figure 1] This will be his guardian spirit's opinion. So, there must be a little difference between what Donald Trump really says in this world, or in the worldly meaning, and what his guardian spirit wants to show him.

Our session may be published in some style and the North Korean people, including Kim Jong-un, will read the contents of this session made into a book, so we must be careful about that. His guardian spirit is thinking about that; he will reveal something,

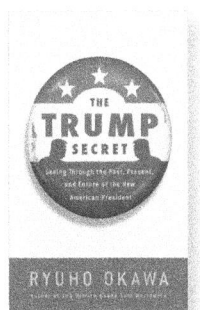

Figure 1.
Ryuho Okawa, *The Trump Secret: Seeing Through the Past, Present, and Future of the New American President* [New York: IRH Press, 2017]

but he is calculating about that, so that even if North Korea knows about that, he can take leadership in the two-countries conference.

Then, is it OK? If possible, I needed a lady because he's very soft at treating ladies, but you are guys, so it's a little difficult for me to introduce him. "Be kind to us," I want to ask him, but he will be a little rigid and difficult, I think. But please try.

Then, I want to summon the guardian spirit of Mr. Donald Trump of the U.S.A.

The guardian spirit of Mr. Donald Trump,

The guardian spirit of Mr. Donald Trump,

Would you come down here?

This is Happy Science General Headquarters, Tokyo.

Donald Trump, would you come down here?

[*About 7 seconds of silence.*]

2

Kim Jong-un Should Say, "We Are Losers"

DONALD TRUMP'S GUARDIAN SPIRIT
Ah...umm [*Coughs.*]

KAZUHIRO ICHIKAWA
Good morning, Mr. Guardian Spirit of Mr. Donald Trump.

TRUMP'S G.S.
Mr. Guardian Spirit? [*Laughs.*] No, no. Please call me "Donald" or "Mr. Trump."

ICHIKAWA
Donald, thank you for coming to Happy Science General Headquarters today.

TRUMP'S G.S.
Yeah, you are my friends, so it's OK.

ICHIKAWA
Thank you so much. Happy Science is supporting you to make America great again.

TRUMP'S G.S.
I know, I know. Thanks a lot.

ICHIKAWA
Though you're quite busy, today, I just want to have a chat with you.

TRUMP'S G.S.
Chat? [*Laughs.*] Just chat. Ah, OK.

ICHIKAWA
Or play cards because you are called Trump.

First of all, we are very concerned about the session between Kim and Moon, Chairman Kim and President Moon.

TRUMP'S G.S.
Uh huh.

ICHIKAWA
First of all, could you tell us your impression on this conference?

TRUMP'S G.S.
In this worldly meaning, it is a progressive result, I think, because I have been quite strong in my attitude toward

North Korea, and this is the result. The essential word is... Mr. Kim Jong-un should say, "We are losers." These are the keywords. We need these words.

But this news indicated that North and South Korea are both in an equal situation and that officially, South Korea admitted the existence of North Korea. So, this is not enough. My intention is beyond this result, but firstly, it's a good thing to make good progress for the better future.

The next conference between Kim Jong-un and me is the most difficult one, I guess so. Ulaanbaatar or Singapore, we must meet and make a conclusion. At yesterday's conference, there was no concrete conclusion or deed shown, and the only clear point was the next meeting between the North and Korea this autumn. This is not enough. So, the crucial decision must be made in these several weeks. I'm preparing for that.

ICHIKAWA
Thank you very much. You said a very important phrase, "Kim Jong-un should say, 'We are losers.'"

TRUMP'S G.S.
Yeah.

ICHIKAWA

But people of the world never think about that because they are making progress toward ending the Korean War and making peace in the peninsula. So, it's very...

TRUMP'S G.S.

Peace and prosperity, they say, but before that, they must admit, "We, North Korea, lost in this war against the international society."

ICHIKAWA

To realize this situation, what would you do for the future?

TRUMP'S G.S.

It depends, but please tell your party (the Happiness Realization Party) president, Shaku...

ICHIKAWA

Ms. Ryoko Shaku?

TRUMP'S G.S.

...Ms. Shaku, that "foolish" Trump would never, ever say that. I'm thinking deeply about that. I'm not so poor at negotiations, so please rely on me. I made up my mind already that they should abandon all nuclear weapons, the long range, middle range and short range missiles, chemical weapons, biological weapons, and other very crucial weapons on the human race. Or else, we will destroy all of their armed systems. We will destroy all of them.

ICHIKAWA

It's very amazing. "Or else, you will destroy their nuclear weapon site"?

TRUMP'S G.S.

Death or give up.

3

What is the First Strategy to A World Full of Democracy?

KIYOSHI SHIMADA
Good morning, Mr. Trump. I just came back from the United States three months ago.

TRUMP'S G.S.
Oh!

SHIMADA
We, Happy Science, have been counting on you...

TRUMP'S G.S.
I know, I know, I know.

SHIMADA
...the biggest example being Master Ryuho Okawa coming to New York and giving a lecture, where he told people, "Mr. Trump will be the president, [See Figure 2]" and it was realized.

TRUMP'S G.S.
Thank you.

SHIMADA

Thank you so much for your decisions and solutions on political issues. As a result, the U.S. economy is getting better and better.

What I'd like to ask is, looking at the situation in the world, Xi Jinping of China and Putin of Russia are ruling their countries as dictators. I believe you are the protector of democracy. What do you see in the future? How would you deal with this situation to make the world full of democracy?

TRUMP'S G.S.

The first strategy is that we must strengthen the treaty between the U.S. and Japan. This is the first strategy. I hope Mr. Abe, or Mr. Abe-like statesman, will lead Japan continuously and we, the two countries, can protect against evil to keep the real democratic system. This is the first thing.

Figure 2.
On October 2nd, 2016, Ryuho Okawa gave a lecture in English, "Freedom, Justice, and Happiness" at Crowne Plaza Times Square Manhattan in New York.

Next is the relationship between the U.S. and the EU. We must keep good ties with the EU because Putin of Russia, I know his ability, but these days, he's changing a little. You said dictatorship. Yeah, really, he has dictatorship. It sometimes means the enemy of democratic system. We need elections.

Of course, Russia has election systems, but in the real meaning, the conclusion is predicted because no one can conquer military power. So, Putin will continue his strong-style dictatorship. He's thinking about rebounding as a superpower. Russia, again, wants to become a superpower. He's trying to protect against the EU because in the EU, several countries have long-distance missiles made by the U.S.A. So, he's very serious about that.

At this point, Syria is the most difficult country. It's the main point of the struggle between the U.S.A. and Russia. It means the Assad regime. How do you think about that? What do you think of the Assad regime? Is this correct or not? He has justice or not? If he is evil, we must destroy his regime. But Russia, they have a friendship between the two countries. There is friendship, so Putin will never forgive our attack. Our attack means, for example, the attack of the U.S., the French, and the U.K.

So, the most difficult problem is if Russia, China, North Korea and South Korea, these four countries want to have some kind of treaty in the military meaning, at that time, Japan and the United States, we two must fight against them. It would trigger Third World War. So, diplomacy is quite, quite difficult from now on, I think.

SHIMADA
Do you think Abe can handle the situation?

TRUMP'S G.S.
I'm the guardian spirit, but we must respect the friendship and personality of Mr. Abe, so I can't say the real thing. Please forgive me about that.

He is a good man. He's continuously seeking for Japanese peace. He has confidence in the United States; its democratic policy and military power. He relies on us, so we want to keep good friendship with him. It's difficult to speak frankly, but to tell the truth, he has nothing to do now. He is at a loss. He is not counted in the world politics today. He is, how do I say, he has a little weak will, I guess.

4

The Deadline for North Korea to Abandon Nuclear Weapons— "Within Three Years"

JIRO AYAORI

So please, let us go back to the problem of North Korea.

TRUMP'S G.S.

Uh huh.

AYAORI

If Kim Jong-un doesn't accept your proposal to destroy nuclear weapons and all types of missiles, will you leave the seat at the meeting?

TRUMP'S G.S.

Hmm? Leave the sea?

ICHIKAWA

If you cannot negotiate with Kim Jong-un, are you going to kick the chair and go back?

TRUMP'S G.S.

Go back... Ah, OK, OK. Yeah, OK [*laughs*]. Not-so-good manner, but it's OK.

ICHIKAWA

It's possible?

TRUMP'S G.S.

Ah, yeah.

ICHIKAWA

Is it one option to leave the negotiation table?

TRUMP'S G.S.

Some people say that I can get Nobel Peace Prize this year, but other people say, "Don't hesitate to attack. Have strong attitude toward him." These two are pushing me. But my strong point is that I, myself [*laughs*], don't know what will happen at the time. This is one of the crazy attitudes, I think.

For example, Mr. Obama can prophesy his opinion or action before the conference. But Donald Trump is the man of mystery, the man of question, the man of [*laughs*] magic. It's my secret power. I, myself, don't know about that; kick the table, kick Kim Jong-un [*audience laugh*], will I give him a suitable punch, or will I just smile at him and shake hands with him? It's unpredictable. Please foresee.

AYAORI

When do you think is the deadline of denuclearization and abandonment of missiles?

TRUMP'S G.S.

When is the deadline? Hmm. It's the most difficult question. They will show some kind of intention to abolish nuclear weapons, but it might be year by year. For example, before the next Tokyo Olympics, they will abandon 20 percent of the nuclear power or weapons, like that. But I don't agree with that. Please show us the total plan of abandoning nuclear weapons and nuclear facilities. At least maybe within three years. Hmm. All of them should be abolished within three years.

AYAORI

In your first term?

TRUMP'S G.S.

Yes! Yes, Yes! That is the condition for my success in the next presidency.

SHIMADA

That means you are meeting Kim Jong-un if some conditions are met beforehand?

TRUMP'S G.S.

In the real meaning, the crucial point is if we support the Kim Jong-un regime or we want to [*laughs and makes a bombing gesture with his hand, but also gestures as if to say that it's a secret*]... I cannot say it in words. We don't want the future of Kim Jong-un regime. I must decide.

Kim Jong-un requires us to guarantee their continuous regime, of course. But the conclusion of the negotiation will make him go into a cage like a tiger which is injured, he will lose political power, or the military will kill him. It depends on the conclusion, but these days, I can say that if I will meet him or not is still 50-50. If, before our session, he strongly issues the prerequisite condition about his protection, I will not meet him. I want to have a free hand. So, please rely on me about that.

5

Trump's Thoughts
On the Unification of Koreas

ICHIKAWA

Thinking about the unification of North and South Koreas, do you agree on the unification of North and South Koreas? Or, do you have any opinions about the Korean Peninsula?

TRUMP'S G.S.

As you already insisted, we must support South Korea. South Korean regime should prevail on North Korea. This kind of unification is permissible. But if North Korea has super-power over South Korea, I cannot admit that situation. So, the conclusion is freedom, equality, no dictatorship, especially military dictatorship, and election system.

AYAORI

The intention of the two, Kim Jong-un and Moon Jae-in, is to create unification on an equal footing. Can you accept that?

TRUMP'S G.S.

It is a weakness of Moon Jae-in, but I cannot control his character. I, myself, have stronger opinion and attitude toward Kim Jong-un, but in the meantime, I must show, or we must show, a welcoming attitude toward peace-making activities for the world.

If we can have a conversation and if, by dint of conversation only, we can denuclearize the Korean Peninsula, and if we can accept the proposal of Mr. Abe, the future will be better. But in reality, we won't have such kind of positive future. We are preparing for the worst situation.

AYAORI

The unification of the South and North means the withdrawal of the U.S. troops from the Korean Peninsula. What do you think of that?

TRUMP'S G.S.

Impossible. Impossible. They, meaning the North Korean military government, will lose their power; this is the conclusion, there is no other choice. They must admit that they are losers. We are not losers and we are not equal. They must know about that. If possible, I can destroy North Korea within three days. We are not equal. They should know that.

But South Korean Moon Jae-in, he is a little weak. If his conversation attitude means that, before his next visit to Pyongyang, he will aid a lot of materials, food and energy to North Korea as a gift, if he is that weak, we will take a more and more strong attitude. I mean, we will go back to the starting point.

ICHIKAWA
You said Mr. Moon is weak.

TRUMP'S G.S.
Weak.

ICHIKAWA
From your viewpoint, what kind of person is he? What do you think about his character?

TRUMP'S G.S.
Moon Jae-in? Just Korean.

ICHIKAWA
Just Korean? What do you expect of him in this matter?

TRUMP'S G.S.
[*Sighs*.] There's one possibility. He wants to solve the problem in a Korean way of thinking. But we,

historically, analyze that these kinds of activities have been mistakes every time. So, he will lose in conversation and negotiation with Kim Jong-un.

Mr. Kim Jong-un is never a peace-maker. He's never a peace-maker. He is the maker of dangerous situations around the east part of Asia. So, he must apologize to South Korean people, Japanese people, and other Asian countries. He should appreciate the cooperation of China and appreciate my smile, I think. He's a bad guy. I think so.

ICHIKAWA
You said dangerous situations in the Korean Peninsula. So, what...

TRUMP'S G.S.
He made it.

ICHIKAWA
Can you foresee the future dangerous situations in East Asia?

TRUMP'S G.S.
Uh huh. Kim Jong-un is thinking that they want to use the power of China and they want to make a balance of power between China and the United States. But now, his analysis is just a mistake. Chinese

Xi Jinping thinks that now, they cannot have military collision with us because China cannot win in that war. If China, Russia, North and South Korea, these four countries have conglomerate power on us, and we lose the relationship between Japan and the United States, at that time, their chance will be 50-50. But now, China doesn't like to make trouble with us, so it's difficult for him.

SHIMADA

We are learning Master Ryuho Okawa's teachings, and one of them says that what's happening in the spiritual world will be realized in this world. So, if Mr. Trump will meet Mr. Kim Jong-un in person in the future, did you, as a guardian spirit, already meet Kim Jong-un's guardian spirit in the spiritual world?

TRUMP'S G.S.

Ah. As you know, I'm one of the gods of the United States. He is not a god, but he is a dictator of North Korea. He is one of the members of Satans in North Korea. I know about that. So, we cannot be real friends.

6

"Japan Should Abandon Relying On Other Countries"

SHIMADA

Thank you so much. Also, Moon Jae-in and Kim Jong-un are influenced by China's Xi Jinping right now. After this, if unification happens, China will increase its power more in East Asia. Do you have any ideas to deal with that situation against China?

TRUMP'S G.S.

I ask Japan to protect yourself in the military meaning, and of course, in the economic meaning and the political meaning. Japan must be the frontline fortress. Japan must have the leadership in the Pacific Rim.

So, I ask Mr. Abe to prepare for China, the total Korean political system and, of course, Russia. We need Japanese military and economic power to keep the peace of the world.

I have another crisis, for example, in Iran, Syria, the EU and Russian relationships, and maybe Egypt or including Israel. There are a lot of future crises in the world. So, we need more power and more wisdom. Japan should abandon just relying on other countries.

Please set up your own system and have suitable or reasonable power. I ask so.

AYAORI
We are *The Liberty*. This is a Japanese magazine. We have some information about your advice to Prime Minister Abe. You demanded him that Japan revise Article 9 and be equipped with nuclear arms and possess aircraft carriers. Did you advise so to Mr. Abe?

TRUMP'S G.S.
Of course, it's the origin of superpower. If you don't have such kind of military powers, you cannot have strong opinion to other countries. Even North Korea, small North Korea, can control you.

You should protect yourself. At that time, we can help you, but if you don't want to protect your own country, and your people, Japanese people, easily want to abandon your nation, your lives and your money or your houses, you easily want to abandon everything, we can do nothing about that. It's your decision, so we cannot protect you. If you want to protect yourself, we will join you and we will help you. But if you want to lose yourself, no one can save or no god can save you.

AYAORI

Last week, we had a spiritual message from Ryotaro Shiba.* He's a famous Japanese author. In the spiritual message, he said President Trump will compromise with Kim Jong-un...

TRUMP'S G.S.

Compromise? Hmm.

AYAORI

...for short-term outcome. What do you think of that?

TRUMP'S G.S.

I sometimes use good words toward my enemy, but it is my negotiation style, so please see all the process. Sometimes I said, "Mr. Kim Jong-un is a smart cookie." It means smart guy. But I just urge him to think of a more peaceful world; if I were his father, I would definitely say so.

It's not just to praise him or compromise with him. I sometimes educate him to have him choose some good conscience within him and want to have

---

* Ryotaro Shiba (1923-1996) A Japanese writer of history. After working at Sankei Shimbun Newspaper, one of the major newspaper in Japan, he became a writer. He won literary award, Naoki prize. He wrote a number of historical novels based on historical heros and great figures of Japan. Many of his works are widely read even now, mainly by businessmen.

him realize that he, himself, has a good spiritual mind in him. It's God-nature, as you say. But in reality, I already decided good and evil. In this point, don't be doubtful about that.

AYAORI
Thank you.

ICHIKAWA
I read in an article on newspaper that the U.S. has decided to send the commander of the Navy, Mr. Harris, half Japanese, as the U.S. ambassador to South Korea. I felt there could be something like a strategy or tactic. What kind of intention do you have about his assignment?

TRUMP'S G.S.
I cannot tell everything. But please believe in me in this point. I will make a great decision and will get [*clap*] a great conclusion [*clap*] within my first period of presidency, I mean four years, at the end of 2020. I will destroy North Korea. They, themselves, self-destroy or I... we will destroy. Both ways are possible, but before 2021, in my presidency, I will make a conclusion.

Even if I lose the next presidential election, nothing can be reversed by that result of the American election. I, myself, will decide and make the conclusion and it means the death of the regime of *evil* North Korea. Then, in my first period, you can see the result. Please believe in me.

7

"I Have No Attachment to Nobel Peace Prize; I Will Do My Justice And Just Depend On My Conscience"

SHIMADA

Is there anything that Happy Science North America or U.S.A. can help you with to fulfill your mission and to continue your presidency? There are many members and people who are in Happy Science U.S.A. Is there anything we can do for you?

TRUMP'S G.S.

Please, please get more members. That's all. I need one million, ten million, or more than that. Can I ask... Oh, forget about that. Forget about that. You don't have enough members and enough political power. If more than 80 percent of the American people know about Happy Science, you are reliable and preferable for me.

In the spiritual meaning, I already rely on you, but in the worldly meaning, your force is not enough. Your forces are not enough. So, more, more members. Please get more, more, hmm... 100 million members, if possible. If it's not possible, then including Canada and the EU, I ask you to get more than 100 million people.

ICHIKAWA

Do you have any message to the American people? Because the next election is coming.

TRUMP'S G.S.

OK. American people, American newspaper, American TV, or American journalist, I don't know what you mean, but I will say I don't have any attachment to Nobel Peace Prize. I will do my justice. I just depend on my own conscience. Nobel Peace Prize cannot change my mind. OK?

I'm not so... I don't use such kind of mean way to get Nobel Peace Prize and win the next presidency. It's "Obaman" policy. I don't like that kind of policy. I am greater than the Swedish and Norwegian people. Haha. Don't think too small of me. I'm a great person and a great soul. I have the mission of God. So, please rely on me.

ICHIKAWA

Thank you very much. In addition to that, do you have any future project or plan in order to make America greater?

TRUMP'S G.S.
Make America greater?

ICHIKAWA
Do you have any future plan or future project for the U.S.A.?

TRUMP'S G.S.
In one meaning, it's economic power. We have trade deficit, so our country needs more international competency in the level of the companies. American great companies spread their power all over the world, but they have no respect to the United States. They must return their profits to the United States. I think so. The enterprises of the United States should prosper more than as they are, of course. We have a lot of military power, but it uses huge budget, of course, so we need balance between that and international trade, and earn more money or profit from unfair countries like China.

Japan also has some problems, but now I say a little about that because we must have strong ties. Through worldwide trading, we want to get more profit, and regarding inner economy, we can change new enterprises and get new jobs and get more income. That will make a strong way to the future.

8

"After the North Korean Problem, I Will Try Changing China"

AYAORI

Could you tell us about the strategy against China? You have started the trade war. What is your intention and what will happen in the near future against China?

TRUMP'S G.S.

They have a large population, but each Chinese person cannot be like an American. So, they have their limits. Because Chinese government has surveillance on their own people. As you said already, they have in the real meaning, no religious freedom and, of course, no political freedom. Only economic freedom, they insist. But this is a bad system. So, I want to change it.

We believe in the power of every person, I mean, the people of the nation. Democracy has its aim. Its aim is to let the people be happier. But in China, people are suppressed by a dictatorship-like government.

So, our next struggle or war just began.

I will change China. This is the next step. If I'm permitted the next presidency, I mean, eight years as a president of the United States, the four years I have left will be to change the political system and the religious system of China. How to change their system including the trade system. So, please rely on me. After I end the North Korean problem, I will try changing China and, of course, changing Russia.

ICHIKAWA

Thank you very much.

AYAORI

You always say that Xi Jinping is a very good man and that you love him [*laughs*].

TRUMP'S G.S.

Xi Jinping is a good person in reality, like Kim Jong-un now.

[*Audience laugh.*]

AYAORI

I understand.

TRUMP'S G.S.

Yeah, a good person. Haha. I have a business mind, so please forgive me.

ICHIKAWA

Now, China is expanding like hegemony in the Pacific area. I heard that they're going to divide the Pacific

Ocean into two at the Hawaiian Islands. We heard that they have a very evil intention.

TRUMP'S G.S.

Uh huh, OK. But Japan will win if Japan can only again compete with China. I hope so. Japan will regain power and compete with China in these 20 or 30 years in the future. I'm not so pessimistic about that.

Oh, OK. We reign within the Hawaiian area. But another area of the Pacific Rim will be controlled by the country of Japan. It's OK. It's enough. I believe in Japanese people. You will succeed again.

ICHIKAWA

Thank you very much for your trust in Japan.

SHIMADA

Economically, I think you will still keep an "America First" policy and strengthen the U.S. economy and fulfill a mission. What is your ideal image of East Asia in the future? How do you see the relationship between East Asia and the United States?

TRUMP'S G.S.

East Asia... I'm thinking East Asia, West Asia, Africa, the EU, and all over the world. It's the position of the president of the United States. I'm thinking about all the world, the Earth, every day. I think about everything. When I want to attack Syria, on the same day, I want to attack North Korea and on the same day, I want to attack Iran.

Can you understand? This is the position or power of the president of the United States.

9

Reforming Islam is a Mission of Happy Science

ICHIKAWA

Moving to the Middle East issues, what do you think about the nuclear agreement around Iran?

TRUMP'S G.S.

Iran. It's very difficult. So, I must finish the North Korean problem as fast as possible. Next problem might be Iran.* They're preparing a nuclear strategy to protect their country from the attack of Israel because I already insisted that Jerusalem should be the center of Israel. They don't accept that. So, they're also thinking about that.

If Iranian people can succeed in preparing a nuclear weapon system, we will need Saudi Arabian nuclear power and maybe Egypt will prepare for the next stage, so the Middle East problem is very difficult.

We should protect Israel. We should keep the peace and keep the profit of Islamic countries. This is the great problem and it will need several more

---

*After this spiritual interview, President Trump announced on May 8, 2018, that the U.S. will withdraw from the Iran nuclear deal agreed to in 2015 between Iran and six world powers (U.S., U.K., Russia, France, China, and Germany), and that the U.S. "will be instituting the highest level of economic sanction."

decades to make a conclusion. So, it's beyond my lifetime in this world.

But [*sighs*] hmm. I think that to protect Israel is essential for the future because Israel is the origin of Christianity. It has the value to be protected. But at the same time, it's also true that Islamic people are important. They should have some restoration or revolution. It means the modernization of political system and economic system. Their religion is too close to politics and economics.

So, it's your mission, the mission of Ryuho Okawa and Happy Science. Please say to them, "Allah changed His mind. Allah is now thinking that politics, economy and religion are different areas, and that the suitable people should study the problem of every area."

In the Arabic area, we need real politicians, or statesmen, and economic-minded people. They should change. They need the EU-like, the United States-like or Japanese-like system. Japan should export its system to the Middle East. You can. Yes, you can. You should try to do that.

10

"Liberty Should Lead to Prosperity And Happiness"

AYAORI

Could you tell us about the idea of liberty because you, President Trump, sometimes say, "the liberty comes from our Creator."

TRUMP'S G.S.

What do you mean by, "the liberty"? Your magazine, or...?

AYAORI

No, no, no, no. Not our magazine. The idea of liberty. Could you explain the idea of liberty?

TRUMP'S G.S.

We are struggling or fighting against countries where liberty is lost or suppressed by dictatorship, like old-style Russia, China, North Korea, Islamic people and some African countries. And of course, the countries which are controlled under the power of gigantic China. So, liberty should lead to the future prosperity and the happiness of the people.

What we should do can be easily found in the area where there is no liberty. That's our job and our mission from God. Americanization should include the mission of God. I think so.

But there also occur religious conflicts and they are very difficult to settle. So, the power would be the power of Happy Science. You need more power than Islam, Christianity or Chinese-like no-God system. You need billions of members. Please fight against your enemies and get more members. I hope so.

11

The Problem and Limit of the EU

ICHIKAWA

Moving to the EU, Europe, I heard you met President Macron of France. What do you think about him?

TRUMP'S G.S.

Oh, yeah, a good man. He's a good man, also. [*Laughs.*] He's a good man. Good man, yeah, good man. Yeah. That's it.

ICHIKAWA

How about Merkel, German Chancellor Merkel?

TRUMP'S G.S.

[*Sighs.*] A little problem... problem. She has a little problem. She might be a cancer of the EU. She is not a dictator, but her influence, political influence is too big in the EU. But she comes from East Germany, so in her brain, there is some kind of old-fashioned Soviet-like thinking or Chinese-like thinking. So, she's logical, but I'm afraid that she doesn't get the real meaning of economic freedom or political freedom.

The EU has its limit. There are a lot of countries to be saved, but there is no strong country that can save them, so the United Kingdom wants to say goodbye to the EU. It has its reason. So, this problem is very difficult.

Macron is a micron [*audience laugh*]. Oh, misfire. Macron... Macron, please change your wife. New model car like me. I changed to a younger wife and I got new source of ideas. He will be expected to marry a younger woman than he is and it will make a new idea, a new wave in Europe.

Merkel already ended her mission. It just means there is no reliable person in the EU. So, America must watch all over the EU.

ICHIKAWA

Thank you very much. Soon, we have to conclude today's session. For the last message, could you show some strong card in your hand to the world? Do you have any secret or plan about politics, economy, or any other matters?

TRUMP'S G.S.

To Japanese people, please rely on me. Don't abandon Mr. Abe at this moment.

I'm reaching China, not to be helped by China, but I'm aiming at changing China soon as the next problem after North Korea. I already understand the problem.

Please work in the U.S.A., "Trump should continue his presidency. He needs four more years. The next president should be Donald Trump. He is younger than he is. He is like 60 years old in power and cleverness." If you are doing activities like that, I love you so much.

ICHIKAWA

Mr. President, thank you very much for today's session. Thank you very much.

TRUMP'S G.S.

Say hello to your followers all over the world. Thank you.

ICHIKAWA

Thank you very much.

[*Claps twice.*]

12

After the Spiritual Interview

RYUHO OKAWA

How is your impression of him?

ICHIKAWA

He's quite wise. He's just pretending to be unwise, but he has ideas, plans and blueprints for the future, so we should trust him.

RYUHO OKAWA

He just wants to say, Ms. Shaku (leader of the Happiness Realization Party), please keep on relying on him. He says so. Well, we'll rely on him. Especially, we'll see in this year, if his personality in this world wants to get the Nobel Peace Prize or not, if he wants to go through the difficulty and get the real result regarding the Korean Peninsula or not. We will see and support him.

We'll make real peace in this east part of Asia and of course, all over the world. We'll struggle. Our political movement will continue.

ABOUT THE AUTHOR

Founder and CEO of Happy Science Group.

Ryuho Okawa was born on July 7th 1956, in Tokushima, Japan. After graduating from the University of Tokyo with a law degree, he joined a Tokyo-based trading house. While working at its New York headquarters, he studied international finance at the Graduate Center of the City University of New York. In 1981, he attained Great Enlightenment and became aware that he is El Cantare with a mission to bring salvation to all humankind.

In 1986, he established Happy Science. It now has members in over 165 countries across the world, with more than 700 branches and temples as well as 10,000 missionary houses around the world.

He has given over 3,400 lectures (of which more than 150 are in English) and published over 3,000 books (of which more than 600 are Spiritual Interview Series), and many are translated into 40 languages. Along with *The Laws of the Sun* and *The Laws Of Messiah*, many of the books have become best sellers or million sellers. To date, Happy Science has produced 25 movies. The original story and original concept were given by the Executive Producer Ryuho Okawa. He has also composed music and written lyrics of over 450 pieces.

Moreover, he is the Founder of Happy Science University and Happy Science Academy (Junior and Senior High School), Founder and President of the Happiness Realization Party, Founder and Honorary Headmaster of Happy Science Institute of Government and Management, Founder of IRH Press Co., Ltd., and the Chairperson of NEW STAR PRODUCTION Co., Ltd. and ARI Production Co., Ltd.

WHAT IS EL CANTARE?

El Cantare means "the Light of the Earth," and is the Supreme God of the Earth who has been guiding humankind since the beginning of Genesis. He is whom Jesus called Father and Muhammad called Allah, and is *Ame-no-Mioya-Gami*, Japanese Father God. Different parts of El Cantare's core consciousness have descended to Earth in the past, once as Alpha and another as Elohim. His branch spirits, such as Shakyamuni Buddha and Hermes, have descended to Earth many times and helped to flourish many civilizations. To unite various religions and to integrate various fields of study in order to build a new civilization on Earth, a part of the core consciousness has descended to Earth as Master Ryuho Okawa.

Alpha is a part of the core consciousness of El Cantare who descended to Earth around 330 million years ago. Alpha preached Earth's Truths to harmonize and unify Earth-born humans and space people who came from other planets.

Elohim is a part of El Cantare's core consciousness who descended to Earth around 150 million years ago. He gave wisdom, mainly on the differences of light and darkness, good and evil.

Ame-no-Mioya-Gami (Japanese Father God) is the Creator God and the Father God who appears in the ancient literature, *Hotsuma Tsutae*. It is believed that He descended on the foothills of Mt. Fuji about 30,000 years ago and built the Fuji dynasty, which is the root of the Japanese civilization. With justice as the central pillar, Ame-no-Mioya-Gami's teachings spread to ancient civilizations of other countries in the world.

Shakyamuni Buddha was born as a prince into the Shakya Clan in India around 2,600 years ago. When he was 29 years old, he renounced the world and sought enlightenment. He later attained Great Enlightenment and founded Buddhism.

Hermes is one of the 12 Olympian gods in Greek mythology, but the spiritual Truth is that he taught the teachings of love and progress around 4,300 years ago that became the origin of the current Western civilization. He is a hero that truly existed.

Ophealis was born in Greece around 6,500 years ago and was the leader who took an expedition to as far as Egypt. He is the God of miracles, prosperity, and arts, and is known as Osiris in the Egyptian mythology.

Rient Arl Croud was born as a king of the ancient Incan Empire around 7,000 years ago and taught about the mysteries of the mind. In the heavenly world, he is responsible for the interactions that take place between various planets.

Thoth was an almighty leader who built the golden age of the Atlantic civilization around 12,000 years ago. In the Egyptian mythology, he is known as god Thoth.

Ra Mu was a leader who built the golden age of the civilization of Mu around 17,000 years ago. As a religious leader and a politician, he ruled by uniting religion and politics.

WHAT IS A SPIRITUAL MESSAGE?

We are all spiritual beings living on this earth. The following is the mechanism behind Master Ryuho Okawa's spiritual messages.

1 You are a spirit

People are born into this world to gain wisdom through various experiences and return to the other world when their lives end. We are all spirits and repeat this cycle in order to refine our souls.

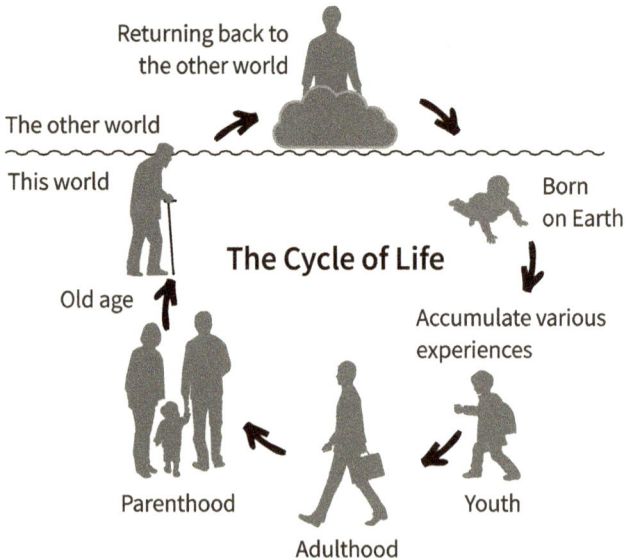

Returning back to the other world

The other world

This world

Born on Earth

The Cycle of Life

Old age

Accumulate various experiences

Parenthood

Youth

Adulthood

2 You have a guardian spirit

Guardian spirits are those who protect the people who are living on this earth. Each of us has a guardian spirit that watches over us and guides us from the other world. They were us in our past life, and are identical in how we think.

The other world

This world

Guardian Spirit

Watches over us/
sends us inspiration

You

3 How spiritual messages work

Master Ryuho Okawa, through his enlightenment, is capable of summoning any spirit from anywhere in the world, including the spirit world.

Master Okawa's way of receiving spiritual messages is fundamentally different from that of other psychic mediums who undergo trances and are thereby completely taken over by the spirits they are channeling.

Master Okawa's attainment of a high level of enlightenment enables him to retain full control of his consciousness and body throughout the duration of the spiritual message. To allow the spirits to express their own thoughts and personalities freely, however, Master Okawa usually softens the dominancy of his consciousness. This way, he is able to keep his own philosophies out of the way and ensure that the spiritual messages are pure expressions of the spirits he is channeling.

Since guardian spirits think at the same subconscious level as the person living on earth, Master Okawa can summon the spirit and find out what the person on earth is actually thinking. If the person has already returned to the other world, the spirit can give messages to the people living on earth through Master Okawa.

Since 2009, many spiritual messages have been openly recorded by Master Okawa and published. Spiritual messages from the guardian spirits of people living today such as Donald Trump, former Japanese Prime Minister Shinzo Abe and Chinese President Xi Jinping, as well as spiritual messages sent from the spirit world by Jesus Christ, Muhammad, Thomas Edison, Mother Teresa, Steve Jobs and Nelson Mandela are just a tiny pack of spiritual messages that were published so far.

Domestically, in Japan, these spiritual messages are being read by a wide range of politicians and mass media, and the high-level contents of these books are delivering an impact even more on politics, news and public opinion. In recent years, there have been spiritual messages recorded in English, and

English translations are being done on the spiritual messages given in Japanese. These have been published overseas, one after another, and have started to shake the world.

1 The guardian spirit / spirit in the other world...

2 Goes inside Master Okawa in this world

3 Master Okawa speaks the words of the guardian spirit / spirit

For more about spiritual messages and a complete list of books in the Spiritual Interview Series, visit okawabooks.com

ABOUT HAPPY SCIENCE

Happy Science is a global movement that empowers individuals to find purpose and spiritual happiness and to share that happiness with their families, societies, and the world. With more than 12 million members around the world, Happy Science aims to increase awareness of spiritual truths and expand our capacity for love, compassion, and joy so that together we can create the kind of world we all wish to live in.

Activities at Happy Science are based on the Principle of Happiness (Love, Wisdom, Self-Reflection, and Progress). This principle embraces worldwide philosophies and beliefs, transcending boundaries of culture and religions.

Love teaches us to give ourselves freely without expecting anything in return; it encompasses giving, nurturing, and forgiving.

Wisdom leads us to the insights of spiritual truths, and opens us to the true meaning of life and the will of God (the universe, the highest power, Buddha).

Self-Reflection brings a mindful, nonjudgmental lens to our thoughts and actions to help us find our truest selves—the essence of our souls—and deepen our connection to the highest power. It helps us attain a clean and peaceful mind and leads us to the right life path.

Progress emphasizes the positive, dynamic aspects of our spiritual growth—actions we can take to manifest and spread happiness around the world. It's a path that not only expands our soul growth, but also furthers the collective potential of the world we live in.

PROGRAMS AND EVENTS

The doors of Happy Science are open to all. We offer a variety of programs and events, including self-exploration and self-growth programs, spiritual seminars, meditation and contemplation sessions, study groups, and book events.

Our programs are designed to:
* Deepen your understanding of your purpose and meaning in life
* Improve your relationships and increase your capacity to love unconditionally
* Attain peace of mind, decrease anxiety and stress, and feel positive
* Gain deeper insights and a broader perspective on the world
* Learn how to overcome life's challenges
   ... and much more.

For more information, visit happy-science.org.

OUR ACTIVITIES

Happy Science does other various activities to provide support for those in need.

◆ **You Are An Angel! General Incorporated Association**

Happy Science has a volunteer network in Japan that encourages and supports children with disabilities as well as their parents and guardians.

◆ **Never Mind School for Truancy**

At 'Never Mind,' we support students who find it very challenging to attend schools in Japan. We also nurture their self-help spirit and power to rebound against obstacles in life based on Master Okawa's teachings and faith.

◆ **"Prevention Against Suicide" Campaign since 2003**

A nationwide campaign to reduce suicides; over 20,000 people commit suicide every year in Japan. "The Suicide Prevention Website-Words of Truth for You-" presents spiritual prescriptions for worries such as depression, lost love, extramarital affairs, bullying and work-related problems, thereby saving many lives.

◆ **Support for Anti-bullying Campaigns**

Happy Science provides support for a group of parents and guardians, Network to Protect Children from Bullying, a general incorporated foundation launched in Japan to end bullying, including those that can even be called a criminal offense. So far, the network received more than 5,000 cases and resolved 90% of them.

◆ **The Golden Age Scholarship**

This scholarship is granted to students who can contribute greatly and bring a hopeful future to the world.

◆ **Success No.1**
Buddha's Truth Afterschool Academy

Happy Science has over 180 classrooms throughout Japan and in several cities around the world that focus on afterschool education for children. The education focuses on faith and morals in addition to supporting children's school studies.

◆ **Angel Plan V**

For children under the age of kindergarten, Happy Science holds classes for nurturing healthy, positive, and creative boys and girls.

◆ **Future Stars Training Department**

The Future Stars Training Department was founded within the Happy Science Media Division with the goal of nurturing talented individuals to become successful in the performing arts and entertainment industry.

◆ **NEW STAR PRODUCTION Co., Ltd.**
ARI Production Co., Ltd.

We have companies to nurture actors and actresses, artists, and vocalists. They are also involved in film production.

CONTACT INFORMATION

Happy Science is a worldwide organization with branches and temples around the globe. For a comprehensive list, visit the worldwide directory at *happy-science.org*. The following are some of the many Happy Science locations:

UNITED STATES AND CANADA

New York
79 Franklin St., New York, NY 10013, USA
Phone: 1-212-343-7972
Fax: 1-212-343-7973
Email: ny@happy-science.org
Website: happyscience-usa.org

New Jersey
66 Hudson St., #2R, Hoboken, NJ 07030, USA
Phone: 1-201-313-0127
Email: nj@happy-science.org
Website: happyscience-usa.org

Chicago
2300 Barrington Rd., Suite #400,
Hoffman Estates, IL 60169, USA
Phone: 1-630-937-3077
Email: chicago@happy-science.org
Website: happyscience-usa.org

Florida
5208 8th St., Zephyrhills, FL 33542, USA
Phone: 1-813-715-0000
Fax: 1-813-715-0010
Email: florida@happy-science.org
Website: happyscience-usa.org

Atlanta
1874 Piedmont Ave., NE Suite 360-C
Atlanta, GA 30324, USA
Phone: 1-404-892-7770
Email: atlanta@happy-science.org
Website: happyscience-usa.org

San Francisco
525 Clinton St.
Redwood City, CA 94062, USA
Phone & Fax: 1-650-363-2777
Email: sf@happy-science.org
Website: happyscience-usa.org

Los Angeles
1590 E. Del Mar Blvd., Pasadena, CA 91106, USA
Phone: 1-626-395-7775
Fax: 1-626-395-7776
Email: la@happy-science.org
Website: happyscience-usa.org

Orange County
16541 Gothard St. Suite 104
Huntington Beach, CA 92647
Phone: 1-714-659-1501
Email: oc@happy-science.org
Website: happyscience-usa.org

San Diego
7841 Balboa Ave. Suite #202
San Diego, CA 92111, USA
Phone: 1-626-395-7775
Fax: 1-626-395-7776
E-mail: sandiego@happy-science.org
Website: happyscience-usa.org

Hawaii
Phone: 1-808-591-9772
Fax: 1-808-591-9776
Email: hi@happy-science.org
Website: happyscience-usa.org

Kauai
3343 Kanakolu Street, Suite 5
Lihue, HI 96766, USA
Phone: 1-808-822-7007
Fax: 1-808-822-6007
Email: kauai-hi@happy-science.org
Website: happyscience-usa.org

Toronto

845 The Queensway
Etobicoke, ON M8Z 1N6, Canada
Phone: 1-416-901-3747
Email: toronto@happy-science.org
Website: happy-science.ca

Vancouver

#201-2607 East 49th Avenue,
Vancouver, BC, V5S 1J9, Canada
Phone: 1-604-437-7735
Fax: 1-604-437-7764
Email: vancouver@happy-science.org
Website: happy-science.ca

INTERNATIONAL

Tokyo

1-6-7 Togoshi, Shinagawa,
Tokyo, 142-0041, Japan
Phone: 81-3-6384-5770
Fax: 81-3-6384-5776
Email: tokyo@happy-science.org
Website: happy-science.org

Seoul

74, Sadang-ro 27-gil,
Dongjak-gu, Seoul, Korea
Phone: 82-2-3478-8777
Fax: 82-2-3478-9777
Email: korea@happy-science.org
Website: happyscience-korea.org

London

3 Margaret St.
London, W1W 8RE United Kingdom
Phone: 44-20-7323-9255
Fax: 44-20-7323-9344
Email: eu@happy-science.org
Website: www.happyscience-uk.org

Taipei

No. 89, Lane 155, Dunhua N. Road,
Songshan District, Taipei City 105, Taiwan
Phone: 886-2-2719-9377
Fax: 886-2-2719-5570
Email: taiwan@happy-science.org
Website: happyscience-tw.org

Sydney

516 Pacific Highway, Lane Cove North,
2066 NSW, Australia
Phone: 61-2-9411-2877
Fax: 61-2-9411-2822
Email: sydney@happy-science.org

Kuala Lumpur

No 22A, Block 2, Jalil Link Jalan Jalil
Jaya 2, Bukit Jalil 57000,
Kuala Lumpur, Malaysia
Phone: 60-3-8998-7877
Fax: 60-3-8998-7977
Email: malaysia@happy-science.org
Website: happyscience.org.my

Sao Paulo

Rua. Domingos de Morais 1154,
Vila Mariana, Sao Paulo SP
CEP 04010-100, Brazil
Phone: 55-11-5088-3800
Email: sp@happy-science.org
Website: happyscience.com.br

Kathmandu

Kathmandu Metropolitan City,
Ward No. 15, Ring Road, Kimdol,
Sitapaila Kathmandu, Nepal
Phone: 977-1-427-2931
Email: nepal@happy-science.org

Jundiai

Rua Congo, 447, Jd. Bonfiglioli
Jundiai-CEP, 13207-340, Brazil
Phone: 55-11-4587-5952
Email: jundiai@happy-science.org

Kampala

Plot 877 Rubaga Road, Kampala
P.O. Box 34130 Kampala, UGANDA
Phone: 256-79-4682-121
Email: uganda@happy-science.org

The Happiness Realization Party (HRP) was founded in May 2009 by Master Ryuho Okawa as part of the Happy Science Group. HRP strives to improve the Japanese society, based on three basic political principles of "freedom, democracy, and faith," and let Japan promote individual and public happiness from Asia to the world as a leader nation.

1) Diplomacy and Security: Protecting Freedom, Democracy, and Faith of Japan and the World from China's Totalitarianism

Japan's current defense system is insufficient against China's expanding hegemony and the threat of North Korea's nuclear missiles. Japan, as the leader of Asia, must strengthen its defense power and promote strategic diplomacy together with the nations which share the values of freedom, democracy, and faith. Further, HRP aims to realize world peace under the leadership of Japan, the nation with the spirit of religious tolerance.

2) Economy: Early economic recovery through utilizing the "wisdom of the private sector"

Economy has been damaged severely by the novel coronavirus originated in China. Many companies have been forced into bankruptcy or out of business. What is needed for economic recovery now is not subsidies and regulations by the government, but policies which can utilize the "wisdom of the private sector."

For more information, visit en.hr-party.jp

HAPPY SCIENCE ACADEMY JUNIOR AND SENIOR HIGH SCHOOL

Happy Science Academy Junior and Senior High School is a boarding school founded with the goal of educating the future leaders of the world who can have a big vision, persevere, and take on new challenges.

Currently, there are two campuses in Japan; the Nasu Main Campus in Tochigi Prefecture, founded in 2010, and the Kansai Campus in Shiga Prefecture, founded in 2013.

Nasu Main Campus

Kansai Campus

HSU HAPPY SCIENCE UNIVERSITY

THE FOUNDING SPIRIT AND THE GOAL OF EDUCATION

Based on the founding philosophy of the university, "Exploration of happiness and the creation of a new civilization," education, research and studies will be provided to help students acquire deep understanding grounded in religious belief and advanced expertise with the objectives of producing "great talents of virtue" who can contribute in a broad-ranging way to serve Japan and the international society.

FACULTIES

Faculty of human happiness

Students in this faculty will pursue liberal arts from various perspectives with a multidisciplinary approach, explore and envision an ideal state of human beings and society.

Faculty of successful management

This faculty aims to realize successful management that helps organizations to create value and wealth for society and to contribute to the happiness and the development of management and employees as well as society as a whole.

Faculty of future creation

Students in this faculty study subjects such as political science, journalism, performing arts and artistic expression, and explore and present new political and cultural models based on truth, goodness and beauty.

Faculty of future industry

This faculty aims to nurture engineers who can resolve various issues facing modern civilization from a technological standpoint and contribute to the creation of new industries of the future.

ABOUT HS PRESS

HS Press is an imprint of IRH Press Co., Ltd. IRH Press Co., Ltd., based in Tokyo, was founded in 1987 as a publishing division of Happy Science. IRH Press publishes religious and spiritual books, journals, magazines and also operates broadcast and film production enterprises. For more information, visit *okawabooks.com*.

Follow us on:

f Facebook: Okawa Books   Instagram: OkawaBooks
▶ Youtube: Okawa Books   Twitter: Okawa Books
𝓟 Pinterest: Okawa Books   g Goodreads: Ryuho Okawa

——— **NEWSLETTER** ———

To receive book related news, promotions and events, please subscribe to our newsletter below.

🔗 eepurl.com/bsMeJj

 ——— **AUDIO / VISUAL MEDIA** ———

YOUTUBE   PODCAST

Introduction of Ryuho Okawa's titles; topics ranging from self-help, current affairs, spirituality, religion, and the universe.

BOOKS BY RYUHO OKAWA

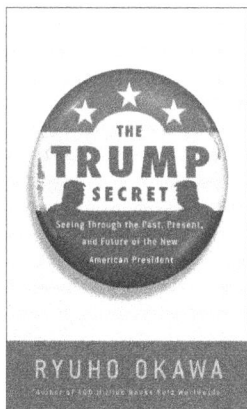

THE TRUMP SECRET
Seeing Through the Past, Present, and Future
of the New American President

Donald Trump's victory in the 2016 presidential election surprised almost all major vote forecasters who predicted Hillary Clinton's victory. But 10 months earlier, in January 2016, Ryuho Okawa, Global Visionary, a renowned spiritual leader, and international best-selling author, had already foreseen Trump's victory. This book contains a series of lectures and interviews that unveil the secrets to Trump's victory and makes predictions of what will happen under his presidency. This book predicts the coming of a new America that will go through a great transformation from the "red and blue states" to the United States.

Contents

Chapter 1: On Victory of Mr. Donald Trump

Chapter 2: Freedom, Justice, and Happiness

Chapter 3: Spiritual Interview with George Washington

Chapter 4: The Trump Card in the United States

For a complete list of books, visit okawabooks.com

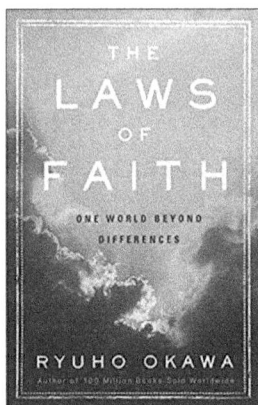

THE LAWS OF FAITH
ONE WORLD BEYOND DIFFERENCES

"Why do people of faith fight each other?" "If there really is a God, then why do war and poverty and other misery occur? "Why does discrimination exist? Are we not equals?" "Did God abandon humanity?" "What is real justice?" "Does God even exist?" This book dives straight into these issues. Ryuho Okawa preaches at the core of a new universal religion from various angles while integrating logical and spiritual viewpoints in mind with current world situations. According to Okawa, it is a misunderstanding that war happens because of religion, and says that deeper understanding for a religion leads to a solution to the problem. He even reveals characteristics and relations of various religions. He also points out the opposition of political values between liberal democratic countries vs socialist totalitarian countries, and the direction the world should head in according to God's justice.

This book offers us the key to accept diversities beyond differences in ethnicity, religion, race, gender, descent, and so on, harmonize the individuals and nations and create a world filled with peace and prosperity.

For a complete list of books, visit okawabooks.com

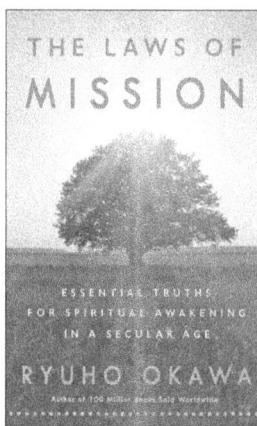

THE LAWS OF MISSION

ESSENTIAL TRUTHS FOR SPIRITUAL AWAKENING IN A SECULAR AGE

In this day and age of advanced scientific and information technology, we are often deluded by a false sense that we know everything. But in fact, many people cannot even answer simple but fundamental questions about life, such as "what's the purpose of our life" and "what happens after death."

In this book, Ryuho Okawa offers integral spiritual truths that bring about spiritual awakening within each of us. This book helps us find the purpose and meaning of our life and make the right decisions so that we can walk on the path to happiness.

For a complete list of books, visit okawabooks.com

THE LAWS OF JUSTICE

HOW WE CAN SOLVE
WORLD CONFLICTS & BRING PEACE

How can we solve conflicts in this world? Why is it that we continue to live in a world of turmoil, when we all wish to live in a world of peace and harmony?

In recent years, we've faced issues that jeopardize international peace and security, including the rise of ISIS, Syrian civil war and refugee crisis, break-off of diplomatic relations between Saudi Arabia and Iran, Russia's annexation of Crimea, China's military expansion, and North Korea's nuclear development.

This book shows what global justice is from a comprehensive perspective of the Supreme God. Becoming aware of this view will let us embrace differences in beliefs, recognize other people's divine nature, and love and forgive one another. It will also become the key to solving the issues we face, whether they're religious, political, societal, economic, or academic, and help the world become a better and safer world for all of us living today.

For a complete list of books, visit okawabooks.com

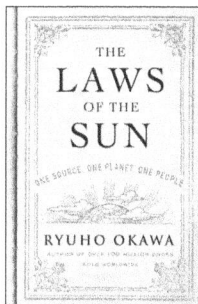

THE LAWS OF THE SUN

ONE SOURCE, ONE PLANET, ONE PEOPLE

IMAGINE IF YOU COULD ASK GOD why He created this world and what spiritual laws He used to shape us—and everything around us. If we could understand His designs and intentions, we could discover what our goals in life should be and whether our actions move us closer to those goals or farther away.

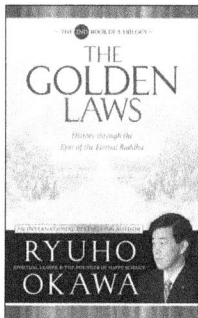

THE GOLDEN LAWS

HISTORY THROUGH
THE EYES OF THE ETERNAL BUDDHA

The Golden Laws reveals how Buddha's Plan has been unfolding on earth, and outlines five thousand years of the secret history of humankind. Once we understand the true course of history, we cannot help but become aware of the significance of our spiritual mission in the present age.

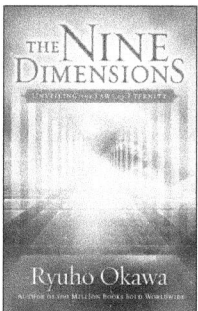

THE NINE DIMENSIONS

UNVEILING THE LAWS OF ETERNITY

This book is a window into the mind of our loving God, who encourages us to grow into greater angels. It reveals His deepest intentions, answering the timely question of why He conceived such a colorful medley of religions, philosophies, sciences, arts, and other forms of expression.

For a complete list of books, visit okawabooks.com

RYUHO OKAWA
FOUNDER OF HAPPY SCIENCE

INTO THE STORM OF
INTERNATIONAL
POLITICS

THE NEW STANDARDS OF THE WORLD ORDER

INTO THE STORM OF INTERNATIONAL POLITICS

THE NEW STANDARDS OF THE WORLD ORDER

The world is now seeking a new idea or a new philosophy that will show the countries with such values the direction they should head in. In this book, Okawa presents new standards of the world order while giving his own analysis on world affairs concerning the U.S., China, Islamic State and others.

1 My Current Opinion on International Politics

2 Indicating Global Trends and the Prospects of a "New World Order"

3 Contentious Issues with South Korea and the Diplomatic Stance Japan Should Adopt

4 The Direction that the Anti-China Demo in Hong Kong is Heading in and Its Effect on the International Community

5 The Future of Islamic State and the Mission of Happy Science

For a complete list of books, visit okawabooks.com

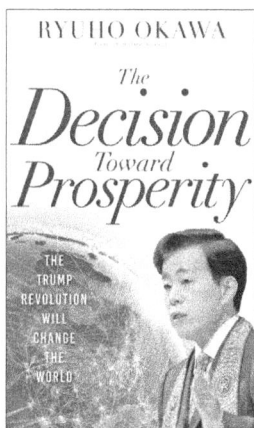

THE DECISION TOWARD PROSPERITY

THE TRUMP REVOLUTION
WILL CHANGE THE WORLD

"Trump Revolution" is a term also used by other authors, not just Ryuho Okawa, but he is one of the authors who see through the essence of this revolution the most. How so? Okawa foresaw the birth of President Trump, as early as in January 2016.

Okawa, a Global Visionary, clearly sees where the world is headed and how the people in each country should think and act for the world to enjoy a better future. As the opinions by experts on American politics or international politics are in disarray, you could say that this book has pointed out the principal pillar of thought.

In the book, Okawa talks a lot about Japanese politics as Japan is his mother country, but the universal philosophy behind his words will surely enlighten readers in other countries, too. This is the guidebook that will help the world realize prosperity for the next 300 years.

For a complete list of books, visit okawabooks.com

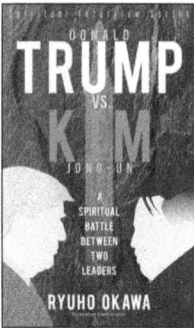

DONALD TRUMP VS. KIM JONG-UN

A SPIRITUAL BATTLE BETWEEN TWO LEADERS

Who will pull the trigger first, Kim Jong-un or Donald Trump? The North Korean issue is entering the final phase. This book tells Kim Jong-un's scenario and the crucial points of Donald Trump's strategy. Here is the top-secret information to the North Korean issue.

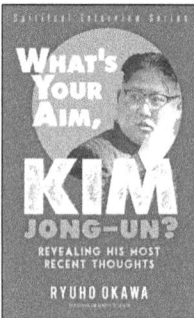

WHAT'S YOUR AIM, KIM JONG-UN?

REVEALING HIS MOST RECENT THOUGHTS

"It would be like a dream if the mass media in the world, including Japan, were permitted to conduct a completely exclusive interview with Kim Jong-un now. Although a spiritual coverage, this book realized over 70% of that wish."

-From the Preface

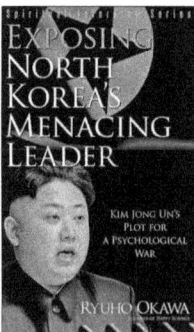

EXPOSING NORTH KOREA'S MENACING LEADER

KIM JONG UN'S PLOT FOR A PSYCHOLOGICAL WAR

This book reveals the role that North Korea is playing in China's imperialistic strategy and the two nations' close ties with Iran. Together, China and Kim Jong Un are carrying out a psychological war that takes full advantage of the weaknesses of Japanese Prime Minister Abe and former United States President Obama.

For a complete list of books, visit okawabooks.com

Spiritual Interview with the Guardian Spirit of New South Korean President Moon Jae-in

The True Intentions Behind his Korean Unification

This book has three chapters, one of which is the spiritual interview with President Moon Jae-in, and subsequent one which reveals his past life. Read this book to find out. It is precious material in predicting the future events.

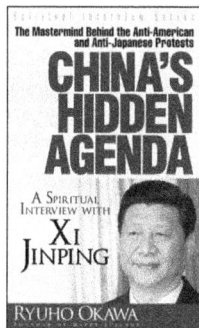

China's Hidden Agenda

The Mastermind Behind the Anti-American and Anti-Japanese Protests

"I wanted to stir up the anti-American movement in the Arab world to make sure that the United States won't be able to attack Syria or Iran...I'm the mastermind behind the Muhammad video."

—Xi Jinping's Guardian Spirit

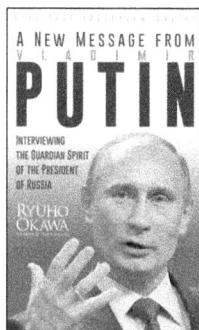

A New Message From Vladimir Putin

Inverviewing the Guardian Spirit of the President of Russia

We hereby bring you the spiritual message from the guardian spirit of President Putin, the politician who is the center of attention of not just the people of Russia but of the whole world, regardless of it being in a good or a bad way. In the Preface, it says, "President Putin's true intentions, which are 90 percent misunderstood."

For a complete list of books, visit okawabooks.com

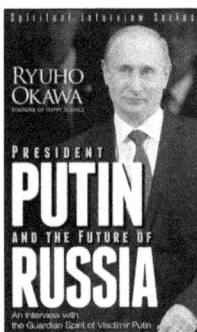

PRESIDENT PUTIN AND THE FUTURE OF RUSSIA

AN INTERVIEW WITH THE GUARDIAN SPIRIT OF VLADIMIR PUTIN

"I have no intention of fighting the United States. The Cold War is over... I have no intention of fighting the Americans... And I'm not friendly enough with China to think about joining them against the United States... I have given Russians religious freedom, which makes me very different from the Chinese."

—Putin's Guardian Spirit

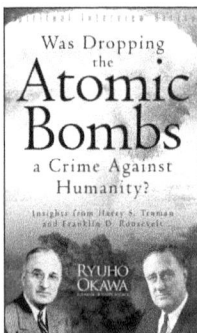

WAS DROPPING THE ATOMIC BOMBS A CRIME AGAINST HUMANITY?

INSIGHTS FROM HARRY S. TRUMAN AND FRANKLIN D. ROOSEVELT

Was there any true justification for the atomic bombing? To answer to this question, Ryuho Okawa conducted spiritual interviews with Truman and Roosevelt. This book reveals valuable information that will help the world gain a truthful understanding of world history.

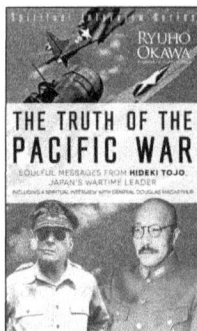

THE TRUTH OF THE PACIFIC WAR

SOULFUL MESSAGES FROM HIDEKI TOJO, JAPAN'S WARTIME LEADER

INCLUDING A SPIRITUAL INTERVIEW WITH GENERAL DOUGLAS MACARTHUR

The material provided is a testimony by General Hideki Tojo, who was Japan's most significant figure in the Pacific War. Furthermore, we have also recorded a testimony by Supreme Commander of the Allied Powers Douglas MacArthur in order to ensure a fair argument.

For a complete list of books, visit okawabooks.com

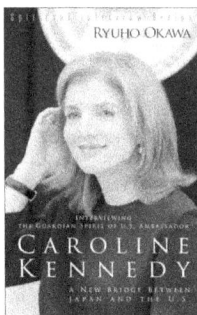

INTERVIEWING THE GUARDIAN SPIRIT OF U.S AMBASSADOR CAROLINE KENNEDY

A NEW BRIDGE BETWEEN JAPAN AND THE U.S.

What is Ambassador Kennedy's views on Japan-U.S. and Japan-China relations? How does she view World War II? What was the reason behind the Kennedy tragedies? What does she seek from the Japanese and American people? Find the answers in this book.

MARGARET THATCHER'S MIRACULOUS MESSAGE

AN INTERVIEW WITH THE IRON LADY 19 HOURS AFTER HER DEATH

On April 9, 2013, just nineteen hours after Margaret Thatcher's death, Okawa summoned her spirit to hold a spiritual interview. Her words will prove helpful not only to the United Kingdom, but also to the global economy and governments all over the world, including those of the United States and the European Union.

THE NEW DIPLOMATIC STRATEGIES OF SIR WINSTON CHURCHILL

A SPIRITUAL INTERVIEW WITH THE FORMER PRIME MINISTER REGARDING THE AGE OF PERSEVERANCE

If there is a chance to hear the opinion of Sir Winston Churchill on current international affairs, journalists around the world will probably be interested to hear this. This book made this possible.

For a complete list of books, visit okawabooks.com

Spiritual Interview with Liu Xiaobo

The Fight for Freedom Continues

On July 21, 2017, 8 days after his death, the spirit of Liu Xiaobo was resurrected to deliver his messages. This book reveals the truths about China, a totalitarian country that doesn't grant freedom to its people. In this book, the Chinese Nobel Prize winner shares his wish to hand down the movement of China's democratization to future generations.

South Korea's Conspiracy

President Park's Hidden Agenda to Unite with China

In this spiritual interview, we begin by speaking with the spirit of An Jung-geun before moving on to a conversation with the guardian spirit of President Park, who forced herself into the interview out of fear that the interview will reveal the truth about him. Okawa hopes that by revealing the truth, these interviews will help the international community understand the nature of true international justice.

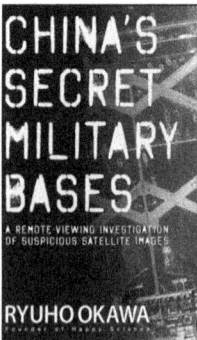

China's Secret Military Bases

A Remote-Viewing Investigation of Suspicious Satellite Images

Okawa reveals China's versions of Area 51 from mysterious satellite photos that had aroused worldwide curiosity. Even American intelligence will be shocked to find out these truths about a hidden enormous missile-launching site full of nuclear warheads prepared to strike major cities around the world.

For a complete list of books, visit okawabooks.com

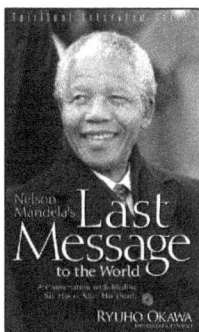

NELSON MANDELA'S LAST MESSAGE TO THE WORLD

A CONVERSATION WITH MADIBA SIX HOURS AFTER HIS DEATH

As Mandela's spirit says in this spiritual interview, God created our souls as thinking energy without color, and that our colorless soul is the basis of our fundamental freedom and equality. In this spiritual interview, Ryuho Okawa gives us a glimpse into the mind of this great leader whose undefeated spirit is a message of hope to us all.

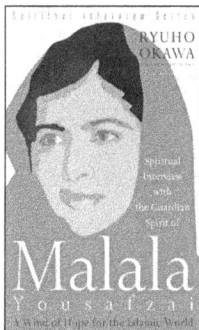

SPIRITUAL INTERVIEW WITH THE GUARDIAN SPIRIT OF MALALA YOUSAFZAI

A WIND OF HOPE FOR THE ISLAMIC WORLD

This is the spiritual interview with the youngest Nobel Peace Prize laureate, Malala Yousafzai's guardian spirit. Learn about where her unyeilding courage and strength springs from and the vision and her vision that she has for the future.

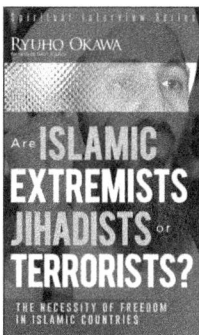

ARE ISLAMIC EXTREMISTS JIHADISTS OR TERRORISTS?

THE NECESSITY OF FREEDOM IN ISLAMIC COUNTRIES

"As the world teacher, it was my duty to determine from a religious perspective whether it is true that the militant Islamic extremists are terrorist organizations, as the West calls them, or whether we should accept them as jihadists of pure faith. I found the answer in this interview."

-From Afterword

For a complete list of books, visit okawabooks.com

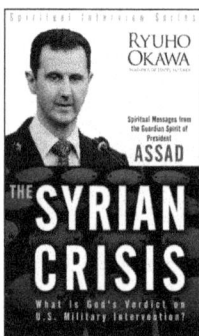

THE SYRIAN CRISIS

WHAT IS GOD'S VERDICT ON U.S. MILITARY INTERVENTION?

As this interview reveals, the Syrian dictator's true character is quite different from what we saw in the CBS interview. As the world braces for a possible world war, Ryuho Okawa provides us with a clear sense of where God's justice lies in this international crisis.

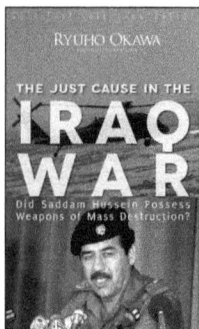

THE JUST CAUSE IN THE IRAQ WAR

DID SADDAM HUSSEIN POSSESS WEAPONS OF MASS DESTRUCTION?

In this book, you will discover that Saddam Hussein was also behind the planning of the 9/11 terrorist attacks and both he and Osama bin Laden are now in Hell. The knowledge this book provides will help each of us make the right decisions as we work together to create a peaceful international society.

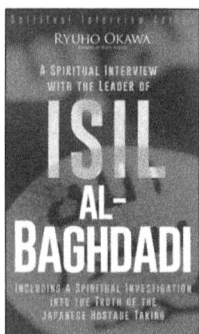

A SPIRITUAL INTERVIEW WITH THE LEADER OF ISIL, AL-BAGHDADI

INCLUDING SPIRITUAL INVESTIGATION INTO THE TRUTH OF THE JAPANESE HOSTAGE TAKING

The author believes we must see through the destiny of ISIL from the viewpoint of world history. Terrorism must not be tolerated, of course—but this book is a precious source to see ISIL in an objective and impartial way.

For a complete list of books, visit okawabooks.com

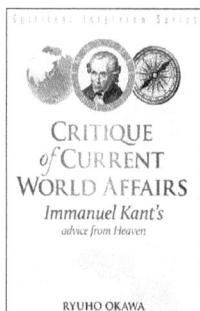

CRITIQUE OF CURRENT WORLD AFFAIRS
IMMANUEL KANT'S ADVICE FROM HEAVEN

"We can clearly see from Kant's message that we constantly need to enlighten people in order to prevent humankind from falling into a dangerous, hellish way of thinking."

-From Preface

[This book is available only in local branches and temples of Happy Science. Please refer to the contact information.]

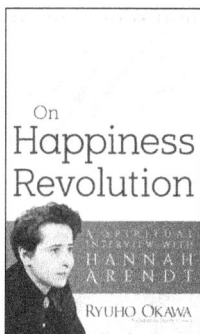

ON HAPPINESS REVOLUTION
A SPIRITUAL INTERVIEW WITH HANNAH ARENDT

In this book, the German-born Jewish American political theorist offers a spiritual lecture on democracy, on totalitarianism in East Asia, on communism and equality, on the Love of God and Justice of God, as well as her mission as a prophet of the new age.

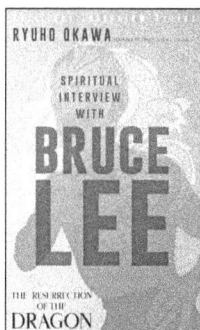

SPIRITUAL INTERVIEW WITH BRUCE LEE
THE RESURRECTION OF THE DRAGON

Here, we present you, martial artists and Bruce Lee fans all over the world who respect him even after his death over 40 years ago, the truth revealed by the "Dragon" who is still fighting evil in the Spirit World. He speaks a lot about his own kung fu philosophy that he had deepened further after his death, as well as the truth of his young death and the mission of his soul.

For a complete list of books, visit okawabooks.com

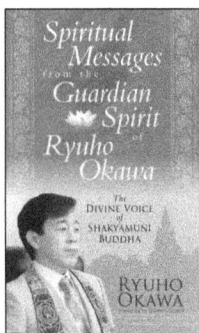

SPIRITUAL MESSAGES FROM GUARDIAN SPIRIT OF RYUHO OKAWA

THE DIVINE VOICE OF SHAKYAMUNI BUDDHA

"The final goal is to realize what you call a 'Buddhaland Utopia.' Of course, this is not an easy task. However, it is important that you keep on making efforts to get close to it, generation after generation."

— Shakyamuni Buddha, Okawa's Guardian spirit

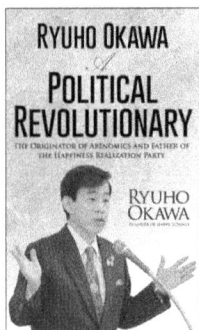

RYUHO OKAWA A POLITICAL REVOLUTIONARY

THE ORIGINATOR OF ABENOMICS AND FATHER OF THE HAPPINESS REALIZATION PARTY

In this book, the Founder of Happy Science Group as well as the Father of Happiness Realization Party, Okawa lays down the guiding principles and the ways to breakthrough on the topics of economy, finance, nuclear power plant, foreign diplomacy, social welfare, and society with aging population and a falling birth rate.

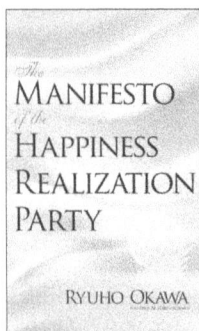

THE MANIFESTO OF THE HAPPINESS REALIZATION PARTY

This book is a historical declaration to change the world through a peaceful revolution by the philosophy and speech based on the Truth, rather than by violence or massacre. It also states on the assessment of the meaning of WWII as well as how the relation between religion and politics should be. It is a must read for all people who wish to build a true utopia.

For a complete list of books, visit okawabooks.com

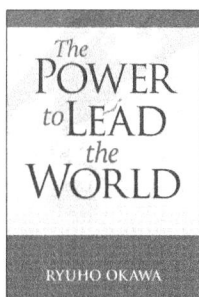

THE POWER TO LEAD THE WORLD

"It is not enough to speak only of ideals; we must envision how this world should be while setting our eyes firmly on things like real politics."

-Ryuho Okawa

[This book is available only in local branches and temples of Happy Science. Please refer to the contact information.]

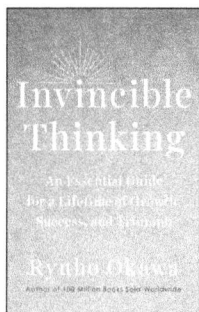

INVINCIBLE THINKING

AN ESSENTIAL GUIDE FOR A LIFETIME OF GROWTH, SUCCESS, AND TRIUMPH

In this book, Ryuho Okawa lays out the principles of invincible thinking that will allow us to achieve long-lasting triumph. This powerful and unique philosophy is not only about becoming successful or achieving our goal in life, but also about building the foundation of life that becomes the basis of our life-long, lasting success and happiness.

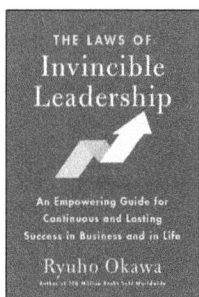

THE LAWS OF INVINCIBLE LEADERSHIP

AN EMPOWERING GUIDE FOR CONTINUOUS AND LASTING SUCCESS IN BUSINESS AND IN LIFE

Ryuho Okawa shares essential principles for all who wish to become invincible managers and leaders in their fields of work, organizations, societies, and nations. Let Okawa's breakthrough management philosophy in this empowering guide help you find the seeds of your future success. Your Keys to becoming an invincible overall winner in life and in business are just pages away.

For a complete list of books, visit okawabooks.com

THE STRONG MIND
THE ART OF BUILDING THE INNER STRENGTH TO OVERCOME LIFE'S DIFFICULTIES

The strong mind is what we need to rise time and again, and to move forward no matter what difficulties we face in life. This book will inspire and empower you to take courage, develop a mature and cultivated heart, and achieve resilience and hardiness so that you can break through the barriers of your limits and keep winning in the battle of your life.

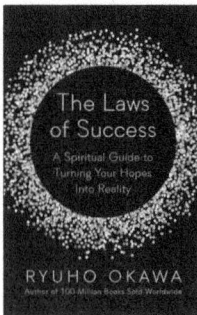

THE LAWS OF SUCCESS
A SPIRITUAL GUIDE TO TURNING YOUR HOPES INTO REALITY

This is a basic introduction to the teachings of Ryuho Okawa, illustrating his core philosophy. He shows you how to free yourself from the suffering of selfish love; how to stop bemoaning your ignorance and learn through study how to cut off negative spiritual influences through self-reflection; and how your strong thoughts will be realized.

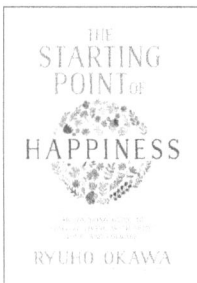

THE STARTING POINT OF HAPPINESS
AN INSPIRING GUIDE TO POSITIVE LIVING WITH FAITH, LOVE, AND COURAGE

In The Starting Point of Happiness, author Ryuho Okawa awakens us to the true spiritual values of our life; he beautifully illustrates, in simple but profound words, how we can find purpose and meaning in life and attain happiness that lasts forever.

For a complete list of books, visit okawabooks.com

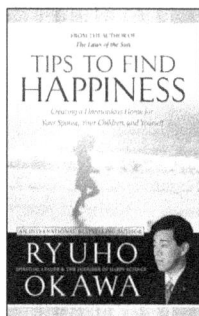

TIPS TO FIND HAPPINESS

CREATING A HARMONIOUS HOME FOR YOUR
SPOUSE, YOUR CHILDREN, AND YOURSELF

This is a series of questions and answers on common problems in marriage, work, and relationships, offering a wide range of both practical and spiritual suggestions that will be sure to resonate with everyone who has experienced difficulties in the home.

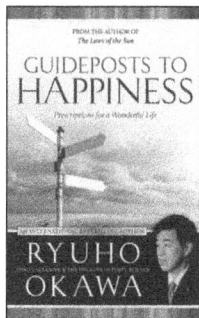

GUIDEPOSTS TO HAPPINESS

PRESCRIPTIONS FOR A WONDERFUL LIFE

In this book, author and spiritual leader Ryuho Okawa describes in detail some of the negative patterns of thinking that keep us from attaining peace of mind. He outlines the causes of a number of life's problems, including depression, inferiority complexes and conflicts that result from over-assertiveness. In this book, you will find many hints to help you solve your worries and attain true happiness.

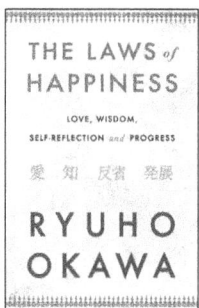

THE LAWS OF HAPPINESS

THE FOUR PRINCIPLES FOR A SUCCESSFUL LIFE

This is a basic introduction to the teachings of Ryuho Okawa, illustrating his core philosophy. He shows you how to free yourself from the suffering of selfish love; how to stop bemoaning your ignorance and learn through study how to cut off negative spiritual influences through self-reflection; and how your strong thoughts will be realized.

For a complete list of books, visit okawabooks.com

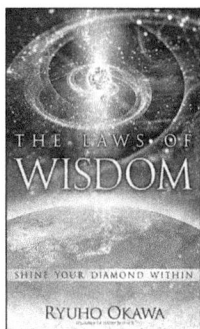

THE LAWS OF WISDOM
SHINE YOUR DIAMOND WITHIN

This book guides you along the path on how to acquire wisdom, so that you can break through any wall you are facing or will confront in your life or in your business. By reading this book, you will be able to avoid getting lost in the flood of information and go beyond the level of just amassing knowledge. You will be able to come up with many great ideas, make effective planning and strategy and develop your leadership skills.

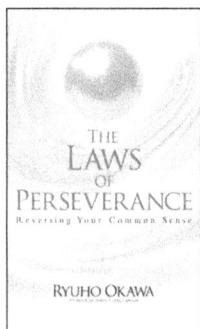

THE LAWS OF PERSEVERANCE
REVERSING YOUR COMMON SENSE

"No matter how much you suffer, the Truth will gradually shine forth as you continue to endure hardships. Therefore, simply strengthen your mind and keep making constant efforts in times of endurance, however ordinary they may be."

-From Postscript

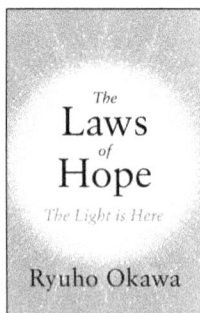

THE LAWS OF HOPE
THE PATH TO YOUR DREAM, SUCCESS, AND MISSION IN LIFE

This book offers various simple tips to find happiness: how to overcome depressed feelings and live happily; how to improve your relationships; how to choose a good life partner; how to achieve your dreams; and how to achieve success in your private life and in your business. By practicing these tips, you can find hope in your future and you, yourself, will be the light to illuminate the world.

For a complete list of books, visit okawabooks.com

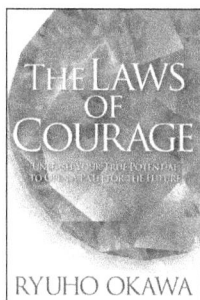

THE LAWS OF COURAGE

UNLEASH YOUR TRUE POTENTIAL TO OPEN A PATH FOR THE FUTURE

In a world of competition and conflict, it is easy to lose sight of who we really are and become overwhelmed by what happens around us. In this book, Ryuho Okawa presents a new perspective to discover a way to live your life with confidence and strength. This book can guide you to a new future for yourself and the world.

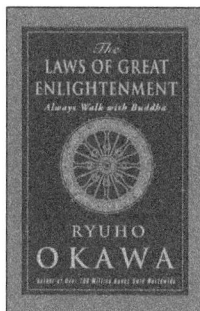

THE LAWS OF GREAT ENLIGHTENMENT

ALWAYS WALK WITH BUDDHA

In this modern society, we often find ourselves unable to forgive someone and maintain a peaceful mind. However, there are ways to lead a stress-free life and enjoy happiness from within. By understanding the Buddhist concept of "enlightenment," you will gain the power to forgive sins and get to know how to be the master of your own mind.

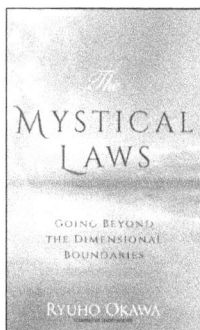

THE MYSTICAL LAWS

GOING BEYOND THE DIMENSIONAL BOUNDARIES

"I believe that once you have finished reading this book, you will find it impossible to return to your old self, for you have now learned the secrets that run through this world and the other.

When you have learned of what has been hidden, will you feel guilt or will you find courage welling up from within? Whichever you experience, you can be sure that the train of life you are riding will take a completely new track."

-From the Afterword

For a complete list of books, visit okawabooks.com

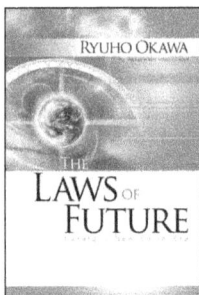

THE LAWS OF FUTURE
HERALD A NEW EARTH ERA

Fight hard for the sake of the future. You must wish, "I will open up a new future, not only for my own sake, but for God's sake, for Buddha's sake, for the sake of my fellow humans with Buddha nature, for the sake of the future of humankind, and for the sake of the world." The road to victory is open before you.

-From Prologue

[This book is available only in local branches and temples. Please refer to the contact information.]

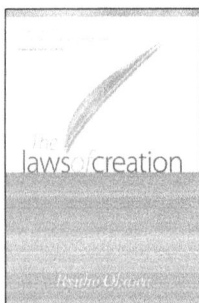

THE LAWS OF SALVATION
FAITH AND THE FUTURE SOCIETY

Why are religions essential to us?

Why should we believe in them?

What is the goal of Happy Science?

–This book will provide you with the answers to these questions.

[This book is available only in local branches and temples. Please refer to the contact information.]

THE LAWS OF CREATION

"No Drop out of the existing "elite track" and create a new one by yourself. This is the true pleasure of life. Respect the weird and strange, and become an honorable eccentric yourself. Be a wonderful eccentric. Be courageous. Become the flag-bearer of the new civilization. Abandon your fearful heart and take on a challenge!"

-From Afterword

[This book is available only in local branches and temples. Please refer to the contact information.]

For a complete list of books, visit okawabooks.com

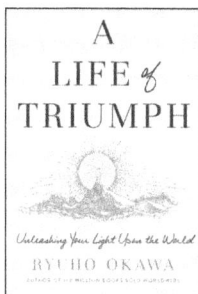

A LIFE OF TRIUMPH

UNLEASHING YOUR LIGHT UPON THE WORLD

There is a power within you that can lift your heart from despair to hope, from hardship to happiness, and from defeat to triumph. In this book, Okawa explains the key attitudes that will help you continuously tap the everlasting reserves of positivity, courage, and energy that are already a part of you so you can realize your dreams and become a wellspring of happiness.

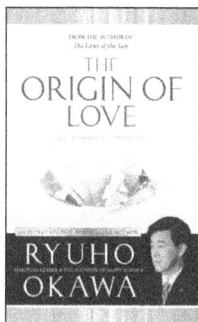

THE ORIGIN OF LOVE

ON THE BEAUTY OF COMPASSION

Why do people love each other, or hate each other? In this book, spiritual teacher Ryuho Okawa answers this question by referring to the origin of love in relation to the secret of eternal life. When you understand the Truth about love, you will be awakened to the wonder of being given life, and you will be filled with love for those around you.

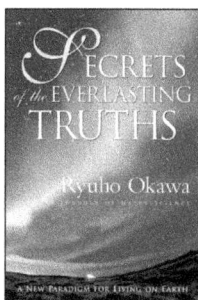

SECRETS OF EVERLASTING TRUTHS

A NEW PARADIGM FOR LIVING ON EARTH

In this book, Okawa shows us an extraordinary array of miracles that are increasing by the day. He reveals the fascinating truth that miracles occur through the help of Heaven and even space-people with whom we Earth-people have shared a very close relationship for millennia. He also shows us a glimpse of the power within knowing the existence of a vaster universe created by God.

For a complete list of books, visit okawabooks.com

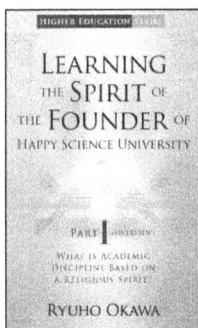

LEARNING THE SPIRIT OF THE FOUNDER OF HAPPY SCIENCE UNIVERSITY PART I (OVERVIEW)

WHAT IS ACADEMIC DISCIPLINE BASED ON A RELIGIOUS SPIRIT?

"The subject of this book is not just for the establishment of the university. It reveals an unwavering set of guiding principles that will serve as a "North Star" for those aspiring to live in a new era." -From Preface

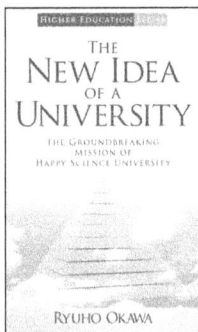

THE NEW IDEA OF A UNIVERSITY

THE GROUNDBREAKING MISSION OF HAPPY SCIENCE UNIVERSITY

In this book, the author and founder of Happy Science University, shares his vision for Happy Science University, a new type of university that has no equivalent anywhere in the world. This book opens new frontiers of academia and that provides clear guidelines for leading the world into a better future.

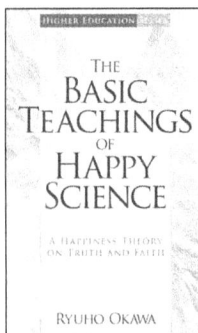

THE BASIC TEACHINGS OF HAPPY SCIENCE

A HAPPINESS THEORY ON TRUTH AND FAITH

When you finish reading this book, three key words, Truth, Faith and Mission that are indispensable to achieve happiness will be left in your heart, and you are bound to discover yourself filled with the wish to live a life of Truth.

For a complete list of books, visit okawabooks.com

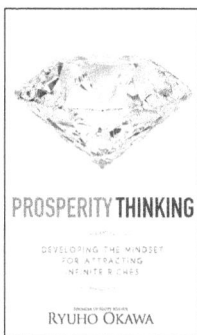

PROSPERITY THINKING

DEVELOPING THE MINDSET FOR ATTRACTING INFINITE RICHES

When you think about wealth, its starting point is to benefit more and more people. Or, put differently, being wealthy is to be appreciated by more and more people. This is the source of wealth.

-From Chapter 2

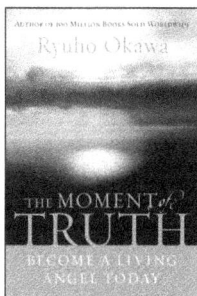

THE MOMENT OF TRUTH

BECOME A LIVING ANGEL TODAY

This book shows that we are essentially spiritual beings and that our true and lasting happiness is not found within the material world but rather in acts of unconditional and selfless love toward the greater world. These pages reveal God's mind, His mercy, and His hope that many of us will become living angels that shine light onto this world.

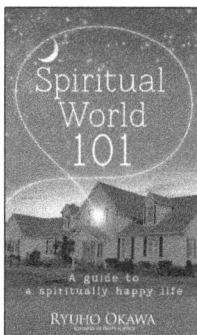

SPIRITUAL WORLD 101

A GUIDE TO A SPIRITUALLY HAPPY LIFE

This book is a spiritual guidebook that will answer all your questions about the spiritual world, with illustrations and diagrams explaining about your guardian spirit and the secrets of God and Buddha. By reading this book, you will be able to understand the true meaning of life and find happiness in everyday life.

For a complete list of books, visit okawabooks.com

MUSIC BY RYUHO OKAWA

El Cantare Ryuho Okawa Original Songs

A song celebrating Lord God

A song celebrating Lord God,
the God of the Earth,
who is beyond a prophet.

DVD
CD

The Water Revolution

English and Chinese version

For the truth and happiness of the 1.4 billion people in China who have no freedom. Love, justice, and sacred rage of God are on this melody that will give you courage to fight to bring peace.

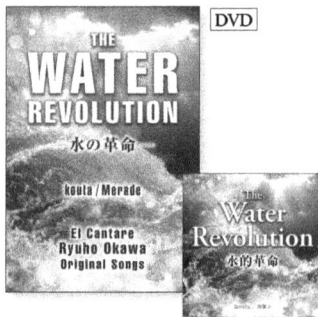

DVD

CD

Search on YouTube

the water revolution 🔍 for a short ad!

Listen now today!

Download from
🎧 **Spotify iTunes Amazon**

With Savior *English version*

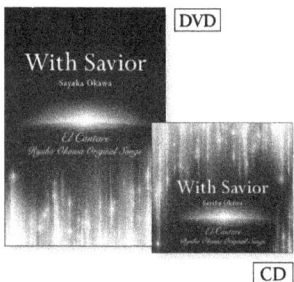

This is the message of hope to the modern people who are living in the midst of the Coronavirus pandemic, natural disasters, economic depression, and other various crises.

Search on YouTube

with savior 🔍 for a short ad!

The Thunder

a composition for repelling the Coronavirus

We have been granted this music from our Lord. It will repel away the novel Coronavirus originated in China. Experience this magnificent powerful music.

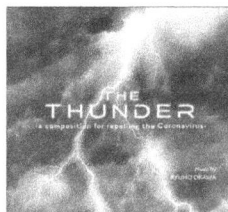

Search on YouTube

the thunder composition 🔍

for a short ad!

The Exorcism

prayer music for repelling Lost Spirits

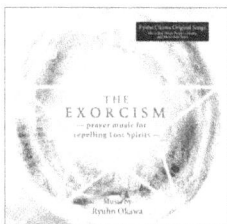

Feel the divine vibrations of this Japanese and Western exorcising symphony to banish all evil possessions you suffer from and to purify your space!

Search on YouTube

the exorcism repelling 🔍

for a short ad!

Listen now today!

Download from

🎧 **Spotify iTunes Amazon**

DVD, CD available at amazon.com, and Happy Science locations worldwide

Notes

Notes

Notes

Notes

Notes

Notes

Notes

Notes

www.ingramcontent.com/pod-product-compliance
Lightning Source LLC
Chambersburg PA
CBHW032057040426
42335CB00036B/441